ALSO BY GALWAY KINNELL

POETRY

What a Kingdom It Was   1960
Flower Herding on Mount Monadnock   1964
Body Rags   1968
First Poems 1946–1954   1971
The Book of Nightmares   1971
The Avenue Bearing the Initial of Christ into the New World:
     Poems 1946–64   1974
Mortal Acts, Mortal Words   1980
Selected Poems   1982
The Past   1985

PROSE

Black Light   1966
Walking Down the Stairs: Selections from Interviews   1978
How the Alligator Missed Breakfast (for children)   1982

TRANSLATIONS

Bitter Victory (novel by René Hardy)   1956
The Poems of François Villon   1965
On the Motion and Immobility of Douve (poems by Yves Bonnefoy)   1968
Lackawanna Elegy (poems by Yvan Goll)   1970
The Poems of François Villon (second version)   1977

EDITION

The Essential Whitman   1988

WHEN ONE HAS LIVED
A LONG TIME ALONE

WHEN ONE HAS LIVED
A LONG TIME ALONE

Galway Kinnell

ALFRED A. KNOPF   NEW YORK   1990

THIS IS A BORZOI BOOK
PUBLISHED BY ALFRED A. KNOPF, INC.

These poems were originally published in the following journals and magazines:

The American Poetry Review: "Flower of Five Blossoms"
Antaeus: "Last Gods"
The Atlantic: "Farewell" and "When One Has Lived a Long Time Alone"
Beloit Poetry Journal: "The Cat"
Boston Review: "Divinity" and "The Vow"
The Georgia Review: "The Massage"
Green Mountains Review: "Agape" and "Who, on Earth"
The Kenyon Review: "The Auction"
The Massachusetts Review: "Street of Gold"
The New York Times: "Oatmeal"
The New Yorker: "Judas-Kiss," "Kilauea" and "The Perch"
The Ohio Review: "The Man on the Hotel Room Bed"
The Partisan Review: "The Ceiling"
Poetry: "Memories of My Father"
The Providence Evening Bulletin: "The Tragedy of Bricks"
The Southern Review: "The Room" and "Shooting Stars"

A limited edition of an early version of "The Auction" and broadsides of "The Vow" and "Divinity" were published by William B. Ewert, Concord, New Hampshire, 1989.

Library of Congress Cataloging-in-Publication Data

Kinnell, Galway
    When one has lived a long time alone
    ISBN 0–394–58856–8—ISBN 0–679–73281–0 (pbk.)
    I. Title.
PS3521.I582W55   1990
811'.54—dc20
                                                        90–53163
                                                        CIP

Manufactured in the United States of America
Published October 18, 1990
Second Printing, December 1990

TO SHARON OLDS

CONTENTS

I

The Tragedy of Bricks   3
Kilauea   6
Memories of My Father   8
The Auction   12
The Massage   16
Judas-Kiss   18
The Man on the Hotel Room Bed   20

II

The Cat   25
Street of Gold   27
Shooting Stars   29
Agape   31
Who, on Earth   33
The Ceiling   36
Oatmeal   37

III

The Perch   41
The Vow   43
The Room   44
Divinity   46
Last Gods   47
Flower of Five Blossoms   49
Farewell   53

IV

When One Has Lived a Long Time Alone   59

PART I

THE TRAGEDY OF BRICKS

I

The twelve-noon whistle groans
its puff of steam high up on the smokestack.
Out of the brickwork the lace-workers
come carrying empty black lunch-stomachs.
The noontime composition consists
of that one blurry bass note
in concert with the tenor of the stomachs.
The used-up lace-worker bicycling past,
who is about a hundred, suctions together mouth-matter,
tongue-hurls it at the gate of the mill, rattles away.
A spot of gold rowels its trajectory
of contempt across a boy's memory.

2

Overhead the sea blows upside down across Rhode Island.
slub clump slub clump
Charlie drops out. Carl steps in.
slub clump
No hitch in the sequence.
Paddy stands down. Otto jumps up.
They say Otto in his lifetime clumped into place seven million bricks,
then fell from the scaffolding,
clump.
slub clump slub clump

Jake takes over from Otto, slubs mortar onto brick, clumps brick onto
    mortar.
Does this. Does it again. Wears out.
Topples over. No pause.
Rene appears. Homer collapses. Angelo springs up. No break in the
    rhythm.
slub clump slub clump
They wear in they wear out.
They lay the bricks that build the mills
that shock the Blackstone River into yellow froth.

3

Here come the joggers.
I am sixty-one. The joggers are approximately very young.
They run for fun through a world where everyone used to lay bricks
    for work.
Their faces tell there is a hell and they will reach it.

4

Fall turns into winter,
poplars stand with their pants down.
The five o'clock whistle blurts.
The lace-workers straggle out again
from under the tragedy of bricks.
Some trudge off,
others sit between disks
of piano wire and wobble into the dusk.

5

A bricklayer walks the roof of the mill.
He carries a lantern, like a father,
which has a tongue in it, which does not speak, like a father.
He is there to make sure no brick fails in its duty.
A boy born among the bricks walks
on packed snow under the walls of the mill.
Under each step the snow sounds
the small crushed shrieks
of the bricklayers, who lie stacked
somewhere hereabout. Suddenly the full moon
lays out across the imperfect world
everything's grave.
From the mill
comes slub clump slub clump. The boy knows
his father and mother will disappear
before the least brick cracks or tells its story,
an antecedence once known as infernal corrosion.
When the boy grows up it will have laid the footing for the concept
    of the neutron bomb.
Which eats first the living forms,
and after that the windows and doors.

KILAUEA

Here is a stone with holes in it,
like a skull. It has furrows,
like my father's brow. Once
he could get up when he wanted and go
into an untouched future; when I knew him
he was sprinting to get to death
before his cares could catch up
and kill him. The small rainbow
that forms around me now curves in,
like the birth-forceps that hoisted me out
—witness the depressions in the temple bones—
until its two ends almost touch
my feet. Could it be that *I*
am the pot of gold? Both pots,
one inside the other,
like the fire leaping inside the steel drum the night workers hold out
    their hands to, in the icy air before morning,
or the pitch-black of speech about to be born through scarlet lips,
or the child getting off her bicycle inside the old woman the priest has
    told to get ready to die,
or the father of Edinburgh rising early inside the son of Pawtucket—
    to whom on Sundays after church he read the funnies, Scripture
    in the father-tongue?
Now the rainbow throws its double onto the air above it—
as on those Sundays, when the first blessing was we were blessed,
and the second, we knew we were blessed.
In the fire pit, where patches
of black skin slide over fiery flesh,

a scrap of paper
the wind, agent
of Providence, tosses in
vanishes without a flame up or crackle—
and my balls, densest concentration of future anywhere in the body,
    suddenly hurt, with the claustrophobia of a million swimmers
    terrified they will never get out.
In the light before dawn
the blue glimmering fades
above four pillows dented all night by four dreaming heads.
The father, already in the cellar,
yanks the great iron lever, the iron teeth
gnash, ashes dotted with fire
crash into the ash pit; and shovels in
a new utopia of coal, in a black field,
which lies quiet, then jets up all over
in flickerings like little senseless bluets.
The pipes and radiators of the house
knock and bang in free un-unison.
In the bathroom he strops the razor,
hoots out last night's portion of disgust,
and shaves, a fleshy, rhythmic rasping, like a katydid's.

MEMORIES OF MY FATHER

1

When we drove a spike too weak into wood too hard
we got, not
the satisfied grunt of everything organized to go downward,
but a sudden yodel,
like a funny bone singing.
I don't want to go back to that workbench
with its smell of spruce sawdust, where the voice
inside things cracks, and changes, ever again.

2

The sound doesn't come from the wheel-rims of the milk wagon
    rattling the milk and the cream down the hard earth of Oswald
    Street,
nor from the ice cream wagon of Peter Pellagi, whose horse, we all
    knew, dropped a horse bun under the wagon whenever Peter
    scooped ice cream inside it,
nor from the cart of the scissors-grinder, who frictioned black steel
    into Faustian sparkles,
nor from the wagon of the iceman, who stabbed out a block of that
    silenced water and lugged it in tongs into the house,
nor from the horse and team of the ragman, who from the next street
    began bellowing his indecipherable cry, possibly "Old rags!" or
    was it just the noise inside things that have turned into old rags,
    "AWWWWRAGHHH!"

The sound comes from none
of these now no ones, but from the no one himself,
the father, who neither brings up the rear nor goes on ahead,
and never rides alongside;
and it approaches closer and closer
and just before arriving goes farther and farther away.

3

In another generation
the father and son come skidding down
the embankment together. They wade
through the shallows, where the bright water
tumbles upon itself making self-licking noises,
then swim to the rock which, like a leak, lets bits of the river fly out.
Everywhere else the water lies flat
and yet seems to slide past faster than other water,
as if there is that force in it
that intimidates matter and can twist
the laws of physics, like the libido inside the lawn bowler's bowling
      ball, which dawdles it along well after it has used up its impetus.
The father and son laugh—unrhythmic, lovely noise—and, as if
      entropy just then curled its tongue inside it, the river cowlicks.
From a town somewhere a consecrated bell knocks
its mild accurate notes all the way to the river.
The boy picks up a pebble, puts it
in the pointed place at the bottom of his pocket,
first checking with a finger for a hole,
then they climb back up
to the path, which, in the schemelessness of things, soon works its
      way back down
to the banks of that secretly frantic water

still shedding its impressions of their bodies,
in which a few, small, horned fishes quietly drift.

4

Can a father give his son
what he himself never possessed,
or lacks the courage to wish up from his own deprivation?
Unlike the boy, who will turn into the father,
and unlike the father, who will turn into no one,
the pebble on the windowsill does not wrinkle, does not die,
though one day it will get lost,
or be thrown out,
maybe by the father the boy who stuck it in his pocket in the first
    place becomes,
when he forgets what it was he wanted the pebble to remember.

5

The motes inside the rays
of sun crossing the room of the childhood house
do not settle but keep turning
through themselves, like the Z° bosons inside matter,
which know the moment they stop they get plucked up,
with a short sucking noise, like a camera shutter capturing a soul,
and belong to the past even before they exist;
in something of the way that childhood happened already;
or like the wedding kiss.

6

When I come back to my father's house,
it will be in any month, though I have loved
fall, and August, and the august moon,
and the moonstruck flagstones going to the door.
When I come back someone will be singing
in an upstairs room, and I will stop
just inside the door to hear who it is,
or is it someone I don't know, singing,
in my father's house, when I come back?

7

Those we love from the first
can't be put aside or forgotten,
after they die they still must be cried
out of existence, tears must make
their erratic runs down the face,
over the fullnesses, into
the craters, confirming,
the absent will not be present,
ever again. Then the lost one
can fling itself outward, its million
moments of presence can scatter
through consciousness freely, like snow
collected overnight on a spruce bough
that in midmorning bursts
into glittering dust in the sunshine.

THE AUCTION

My wife lies in another dream.
The quilt covers her like a hill
of neat farms, or map of the township
that is in heaven, each field and pasture
its own color and sufficiency,
every farm signed in thread
by a bee-angel of those afternoons,
the tracks of her inner wandering.
In this bed spooled out of rock maple plucked
from the slopes above the farm, saints
have lain side by side, grinding their
teeth square through the winter nights,
or tangled together, the swollen
flesh finding among the gigantic
sleep-rags the wet vestibule, jetting
milky spurts into the vessel
as secret as that amethyst glass
glimpsed once overlaid with dust
in the corner of an attic.

2

Their babies have cried
their winter mornings
in this crib that rocks

calm into the jumble and holds
a woman-child the size of a peck
of onions, who still sleeps,
the lump of freestone
still warm at her feet,
under her own small hill.

3

Out now
in the cold air, under
the fading moon—the lithe-handled axe,
which has arrived like a guillotine
on the cords that tie up the brain-bags
of hen, wreaks down on maple-halves
harder to drive apart than
faithful lovers.

4

The fire inside the potbellied
stove wallows and sighs, blood of the
swollen iron of this squat god puffed up
and dreaming of smoke and waste-laying—
where the laid-out body of hen sweated grease
and freestone soaked up heat for the long night
and exhalations of small creatures bloated the globby batches in the
    shining pans,
and fire waved, in secret, jets of remembrance
out of the cloven
wood.

5

Rinse of ocher and lampblack
and skimmed milk drench the chest picked up
at the Federated Church auction the color of blood
spilled long ago—*All the old love letters
go with it, all go!*—this box-load
of antique affections whose bonds lie among sleepers
in the scythed, white-fenced precinct
on the Heights, their alphabets
now two scatterings of bones—
of a farmer who slew
the great trees and touched them to flames,
and dragged stones off their glacial graves,
and each dawn and each dusk squeezed
the alembicked juice of vetch and alfalfa into the barking pail bottom,
and of a farm wife
who sat in the dim parlor, easing
the spurting sorrow-milks of narrow rooms,
who touched the keys and trampled
the Holy Ghost into the machinery, and poured
Faith of Our Fathers
into the heavy Sunday, shifting
from Claribel to Dulciana to Vox Jubilante
to Vox Humana, where all the stops end,
saturating the air with such yearning
no one can sing it until the day when, crushed under
scored pistons on freeways not yet imagined,
exploded in oil, it comes back,
poisoned, purged of transcendence forever.
All the love letters go with it, all go.

6

On the shelf stands
a hand-blown whisky bottle
from the old days, blown askew
by the gray lungs of the Czechoslovak,
which a farmer—after a week
of dragging stones into the error
of walls, of squeezing and resqueezing
the exuberance of udders into
the squawking foam, of smiting
maple and ash into flame-chunks—
seized and doled to himself
in slow swigs through most of a Sunday,
lying at last stunned in the vapors
of corn-sap steamed from the rock-sucking fields,
while the jubilant pipes jetted Faith
of Our Fathers into the darkened house—
and so drank out his wandering.

7

These farm shoes by the door,
covered in dried mud, a hobnail
or two touched by first light,
hold the shapes a man trudged
into them a last time before dawn,
going out the other end of the barn,
straying across the pasture, climbing
all the way to the sugarbush
most of it sold off to the spindle mill,
passing beneath an owl, startling a few doves,
to see the sun come up.

THE MASSAGE

Hoisted onto the table, he lies limp.
He likes this—existence annihilated
into these two hands. How could anyone
willingly leave a world where they touch you
all over your body? He can almost feel
the hard skin, the crooked last
finger-joints—no one has touched him
so unstintingly since she unsafety-pinned
and talcum-slicked the tiny little body.
Only the hands of the hitter do not tire.
They alone know how to whack from deep down
the big double-salted tears that, licked
into the mouth, taste of the soul,
maybe the whiff of amniotic fluid once
at the birth-table. He lies bunched up,
in a corner, in remorse, eyes squeezed shut
and a tear popping out, like the tongue
of a snake through its closed smile.
The hands find coagulated rump-tissue—delve,
spear, grabble, until the buttocks want to jig.
He can hear a humming—the awakening
inside a teakettle, that will shriek
when hot enough to make its peaceful drink,
or the blades flinching away from each other overhead,
or the noises ironed flat in the horizontal plane
back in the kitchen where the sharp tongue
made its points while she puttered about,
that he was dumb, that he was worthless,

that he would never reach the future alone.
A siren struggles in the distance—maybe
an ambulance out prowling for a new geezer
to throw on the table and stroke, until he ramps,
and then agrees to croak. The hands separate
his hands into their fingers, using the tugs
of the sandwich-maker after Thanksgiving, who pries
flesh off little brown unidentifiable bones
of the creature who days before clomped about
abruptly gobbling as though thinking up jokes.
Far down inside his chest it feels sore.
The hands can't pass the twelve cartilaginous bars.
The future he dreaded seems to have dissolved
on approach, and reassembled behind as the past—
but slightly blurred, being mostly unlived.
The hands disappear. The horns of cars,
and a more urgent siren, possibly the police,
or a fire, touch through. The cadaver
two beds away spits out the scatological verbs,
as though he fears they will frisk his heart
in the next world. Through the wall,
from the next ward, come hard, uninhibited groans.

JUDAS-KISS

Those who lie waiting know time
goes away eventually but in the meantime
sits there—oh maybe shuffles in its mechanisms
once in a while, skips a day, sometimes
behind you a whole year can get lost,
but basically sits there. Hair doesn't
turn white, skin refuses to mat
its spidery crushings over
the face-bones, the tiny ditched
carcasses of remembered acts
remain stuck nose and feet
to the amberish helix
of the heaven of childhood,
which droops down into the golden ringlet
of hell. Most can wait
for the capsule's slow burst
to lull them off, but some, dying
to get on with it, swill the whole
bottle-load down in one
foul gulp. Then somebody,
an ex-spouse, the woman downstairs,
or maybe the UPS man, will happen by,
discover the collapsed creature,
and never mind if it sleeps through
its last clutches, bend down,
and with the softest
part of the face, which hides
the hardest, Judas-kiss it,

with a click, like a conductor's
ticket-punch, this one here, God
of our Fathers, this one is the one.

THE MAN ON THE HOTEL ROOM BED

He shifts on the bed carefully, so as
not to press through the first layer
into the second, which is permanently sore.
For him sleep means lying as still as possible
for as long as possible thinking the worst.
Nor does it help to outlast the night—
in seconds after the light comes
the inner darkness falls over everything.
He wonders if the left hand of the woman
in the print hanging in the dark above the bed,
who sits half turned away, her right hand
clutching her face, lies empty,
or does it move in the hair of a man
who dies, or perhaps died long ago
and sometimes comes and puts his head in her lap,
and then goes back and lies under a sign
in a field filled nearly up to the roots
holding down the hardly ever trampled grass
with mortals, the once-lovers. He goes over
the mathematics of lying awake all night alone
in a strange room: still the equations require
multiplication, by fear, of what is,
to the power of desire. He feels around—
no pillow next to his, no depression
in the pillow, no head in the depression.
Love is the religion that bereaves the bereft.
No doubt his mother's arms still waver up
somewhere reaching for him; and perhaps

his father's are now ready to gather him
there where peace and death dangerously mingle.
But the arms of prayer, which pressed his chest
in childhood—long ago, he himself, in the name
of truth, let them go slack. He lies facedown,
like something washed up. Out the window
first light pinks the glass building across
the street. In the religion of love to pray
is to pass, by a shining word, into the inner chamber
of the other. It is to ask the father and mother
to return and be forgiven. But in this religion
not everyone can pray—least of all
a man lying alone to avoid being abandoned,
who wants to die to escape the meeting with death.
The final second strikes. On the glass wall
the daylight grows so bright the man sees
the next darkness already forming inside it.

PART II

THE CAT

The first thing that happened
was that somebody borrowed the Jeep,
drove fifty feet, went off the road.
The cat may have stuck a tire iron
or baseball bat into the steering wheel.
I don't know if it did or didn't.
I do know—I don't dare say it aloud—
when the cat is around something goes wrong.
Why doesn't our host forewarn us? Well,
he tries. He gives each guest on arrival
a list of instructions about the cat.
I never was able to read mine,
for the cat was watching when I got it,
so I stuck it in my pocket to read later,
but the cat saw, leapt at me, nearly
knocked me down, clawed at the pocket,
would have ripped my clothes off
if I had not handed it over.
The guest book contains the name
of the young woman who was my friend,
who brought me here in the first place,
who is the reason I have come back,
to find out what became of her.
But no one would tell me anything.
Except tonight, my final evening,
at dinner, the host says, "There is
someone . . . someone . . . a woman . . .
in your life . . ." I know he means her,

but why the present tense? "Whom you have in . . ."
The next word sounds like "blurrarree"
but it could be "slavery." "Well, yes,"
I say. "Yes, but where is the cat?"
"It is an awful thing you are doing,"
he goes on. "Quite awful." "But who?"
I protest. "What are you talking about?"
"The cat," he says. "When you lock her up
she becomes dangerous." "The cat?
What cat?" I remember the kitten I saved
out of the burlap sack when I was seven,
I was fathering or mothering her, my father
or mother said, "Stop smothering it."
Suddenly an electric force grabs my feet.
I see it has seized the host too—
he is standing up, his hands are flopping
at his sides. "What is it?" I whisper.
"I'm washing the dishes," he says.
"O my God," I think.
"I'm washing the dishes," he repeats.
I realize he is trying to get the cat to believe
he is not in a seizure but washing the dishes.
If either of us lets on about the seizure
I know for certain the cat will kill us both.

STREET OF GOLD

When I step forward to go to her
the concrete turns mushy and I sink in;
then it sets. Maybe she too stands
on a sidewalk somewhere, feet stuck.
More likely she sits on her bed,
bent forward, brushing yellow hair
over her head. If a few strands could
escape and blow here, that would be how
the wind passing under the streetlight
gets its glitter. A woman folds up
for the night on the bank steps,
a man works himself feet first into
a cardboard box—without a bedfellow,
or a face doughy from cold nights
a face could nuzzle. A bottle a passer
kicks into the street goes spinning across
the cobblestones' falsetto notes.
In a great hall a countertenor
rises up on tiptoe, opens his throat,
unspoons them into heaven. The bottle
chucks the cobblestones' fat cheeks.
A little girl wakes to ecstatic murder
taking place in some guttural language,
runs, peeks, watches a man and woman,
steady as a backyard oil jack,
pumping her back down into nonexistence.
A strand of yellow hair hits my forehead,
presses across it a familiar double-humped wobble.

The bottle stops. The man in the box
gropes in his fly, finds only a worm.
The woman on the steps finds a dry well
under the wilful hair. The wind turns cold.
The cobblestones soon will be rattling
in their sockets. What's going to happen?
Some will stay put. Some will change sleeping streets,
some will disappear for a stricter reason.
Enough will get bumped from home to replace them.
She will fly to California and marry.
The night runs out of gold. And I
am almost as old as my father.

SHOOTING STARS

It's empty, blank blue
up there, the sun's violent light
flies right through. Last night,
my God, the shooting stars!
The sky brilliant with them,
with meteors lined up, speeding
toward earth!—of which only
a few arrive unburned-up
into this swarm of lover
tangled upon lover. Yesterday,
because of the P-rade
(my G-d, can even p,a,r,a,d,e
form the Tetragrammaton?),
Nassau Street, too, was thronged,
as the graduated classes
passed in historical order—
first a solitary scout,
then a few stragglers, then
ever-larger bands
of rickety, well-wattled
old timers—including
my old friends and old strangers
of '48, all decked out
in black and orange
like rocket men. Last night,
deaths up there more brilliant
than lives—the way
they see us on the other side,

when we come through, red-faced,
cries foremost, as at birth,
still breathing heavily
from the hard labor
of dying. But today
it is clear again up there,
the escape-holes blued over,
the litter of scorched itineraries
broomed up. It is time for her
to go, who came down
from elsewhere, toward me
—startling herself,
not having guessed she could
crave love or take joy in it
so desperately—who is
by now an adept and could pluck
drunken flesh off a sidewalk
and with a kiss, or a
flurrying of lips at an ear,
come up with Adonis—
time to forget
about the criss . . . crissing
of earthly and heavenly bodies
torching each other
into bliss. On Nassau Street,
vacuumed, plucked of lint, again
the almost-black of the thick,
practically still wet flannel
of preachers' trousers, a man dressed
in the colors of soot and fire,
who last night could have flamed in inhuman arms,
imagined himself a god, staggers,
looking for the way out of here.

AGAPE

I want to touch her.
Once. Again. I will wait
if I must. Outwait.
Wait so long she will age,
pull even, pass. How
will she like it then if
when I bend to kiss wrinkles
ray out around her
mouth? I want to hold her.
In the flesh. All night.
Flesh like the bright
puffs the flower-god
puts on in spring, flimsy
for needing to last
but this one flashing
circuit through her
apparitions. Did she fear,
when I stood with the
precipice at my back
and beckoned, that I was a specter
she would plunge through?
At the agape love's addicts
lie back, drink, listen
to a priestess discourse
on love rightly understood.
As soon as cured anyone
can get up and go over
and bestow the Kiss

on anyone. Now the others
have disappeared—maybe
cured, probably joining lips
behind doors. It is
the Fourth Cup—the hour
for the breaking of the
transubstantiated body.
What if we break, the priestess
and I, the body
together? And I fall
in fear and longing? And
she commands me to
dissolve in the light
of love rightly understood,
or if I can't, to put
a gun to my head? I don't want
to know that on the other
side of the pillow nobody
stirs. I don't want ever
again to sit up half the night
and laugh and forget not
all of us will rejoice
like this always.

WHO, ON EARTH

A ship sits on the sea raking
the water for fishes. A wave
flops heavily on top
of itself, defeat, and before
long does it again, defeat.
A skate, a baby, newly beached,
lies on the sand working her
sucking holes. Last night
I woke to a singing so high
it used only a soprano's
last outer notes, sometimes
sliding up into ultra-alts—
music a whale straying
into the Aegean long ago
might have keened through the wood walls
of ships in the black hours,
luring, wrecking
the sailors. I followed
down dark corridors to a lighted
courtyard where a woman sat
up to her waist in a pool,
singing. She turned
and kept singing, as though
she saw someone through me
and sang to him. Her breasts
were small and shapely,
like an athlete's, their
nipples never darkened

by the remorseless mouths
of babies. On the blurred
flesh under water black
dulse stirred—and down there too
was a sparkling, as of scales,
as if the submerged half of her
might be shutting itself up now
inside a fish tail—or, it could be,
pipping, busting, uncrumpling
a forked creature. On the beach,
pebbles, or maybe scales
shed on this spot at high tide
in some throe of metamorphosis,
gleam. In the skate
the mass of whatever
substance flesh on dying becomes
presses down into the sand,
trying to fall into the heaven
inside earth almost visible
through the half-washed windows
of stones. The sea
bristles up in waves. The largest
strikes the shore, gets upended,
leaps, lunges, crawls
all the way up to the skate,
then half sinking straight down,
half flowing back out, drags off
the carcass, leaving bubbles,
which pop, leaving the force
that crushes waves into nothing
to its victory. As when
mom harangues and pop icy-shoulders
the boy who can't think, can't yell,

34

explain himself, laugh, love, or sing;
can only fall in loneliness
with . . . but . . . who,
on earth?

THE CEILING

I don't like looking at
this ceiling of sprayed concrete
that would scrape the will out of anyone
who had decided to rise and pass through—just as
the trompe l'oeil of jagged rocks
on the Elmer Holmes Bobst Library floor
conjures up shattered flesh
in someone thinking of climbing over
those protruding balusters—
cruciform steel rods baring their row
of sharp crosses along the top, to interdict
the Christians, and make others imagine
being speared and hooked up halfway over.
But I don't want to wake up under
the smooth-plastered ceiling of my childhood either—
its cracks showed me the way but did not tell me the price.
A mild-spoken, uneasy man in a white jacket speaks
of Elavil, Lithane, Norpramin, Prozac, Desyrel, Xanax.
The woman with black eyes puts
the wafer she spirited out of Mass
under my pillow—scored with a Cross,
it will come apart into four, under
my heavy head, when we tumble,
or toss. I want a kiss
from red lips, like lip-petals in a garden,
speaking I don't know what to the morning.
I don't want to die.
I want to be born.

OATMEAL

I eat oatmeal for breakfast.

I make it on the hot plate and put skimmed milk on it.

I eat it alone.

I am aware it is not good to eat oatmeal alone.

Its consistency is such that it is better for your mental health if
somebody eats it with you.

That is why I often think up an imaginary companion to have
breakfast with.

Possibly it is even worse to eat oatmeal with an imaginary companion.

Nevertheless, yesterday morning, I ate my oatmeal—porridge, as he
called it—with John Keats.

Keats said I was absolutely right to invite him: due to its glutinous
texture, gluey lumpishness, hint of slime, and unusual willingness
to disintegrate, oatmeal must never be eaten alone.

He said that in his opinion, however, it is perfectly OK to eat it with
an imaginary companion,

and he himself had enjoyed memorable porridges with Edmund
Spenser and John Milton.

Even if eating oatmeal with an imaginary companion is not as
wholesome as Keats claims, still, you can learn something from it.

Yesterday morning, for instance, Keats told me about writing the
"Ode to a Nightingale."

He had a heck of a time finishing it—those were his words—"Oi 'ad
a 'eck of a toime," he said, more or less, speaking through his
porridge.

He wrote it quickly, on scraps of paper, which he then stuck in his
pocket,

but when he got home he couldn't figure out the order of the stanzas,
and he and a friend spread the papers on a table, and they made
some sense of them, but he isn't sure to this day if they got it right.
An entire stanza may have slipped into the lining of his jacket through
a hole in the pocket.
He still wonders about the occasional sense of drift between stanzas,
and the way here and there a line will go into the configuration of a
Moslem at prayer, then raise itself up and peer about, and then lay
itself down slightly off the mark, causing the poem to move
forward with God's reckless wobble.
He said someone told him that later in life Wordsworth heard about
the scraps of paper on the table, and tried shuffling some stanzas
of his own, but only made matters worse.
I would not have known about any of this but for my reluctance to eat
oatmeal alone.
When breakfast was over, John recited "To Autumn."
He recited it slowly, with much feeling, and he articulated the words
lovingly, and his odd accent sounded sweet.
He didn't offer the story of writing "To Autumn," I doubt if there is
much of one.
But he did say the sight of a just-harvested oat field got him started
on it,
and two of the lines, "For Summer has o'er-brimmed their clammy
cells" and "Thou watchest the last oozings hours by hours," came
to him while eating oatmeal alone.
I can see him—drawing a spoon through the stuff, gazing into the
glimmering furrows, muttering—and it occurs to me:
maybe there is no sublime; only the shining of the amnion's tatters.
For supper tonight I am going to have a baked potato left over from
lunch.
I am aware that a leftover baked potato is damp, slippery, and
simultaneously gummy and crumbly,
and therefore I'm going to invite Patrick Kavanagh to join me.

PART III

THE PERCH

There is a fork in a branch
of an ancient, enormous maple,
one of a grove of such trees,
where I climb sometimes and sit and look out
over miles of valleys and low hills.
Today on skis I took a friend
to show her the trees. We set out
down the road, turned in at
the lane which a few weeks ago,
when the trees were almost empty
and the November snows had not yet come,
lay thickly covered in bright red
and yellow leaves, crossed the swamp,
passed the cellar hole holding
the remains of the 1880 farmhouse
that slid down into it by stages
during the forties, followed
the overgrown logging road
and came to the trees. I climbed up
to the perch, and this time looked
not into the distance but at
the tree itself, its trunk
contorted by the terrible struggles
of that time when it had its hard time.
After the trauma it grows less solid.
It may be some such time now comes upon me.
It would have to do with the unaccomplished,
and with the attempted marriage

of solitude and happiness. Then a rifle
sounded, several times, quite loud,
from across the valley, percussions
of the custom of male mastery
over the earth—the most graceful,
most alert, most gentle of the animals
being chosen to die. I looked
to see if my friend had heard,
but she was stepping about on her skis,
studying the trees, smiling to herself,
her lips still filled, for all
we had drained them, with hundreds
and thousands of kisses. Just then
she looked up—the way, from low
to high, the god blesses—and the blue
of her eyes shone out of the black
and white of bark and snow, as lovers
who are walking on a freezing day
touch icy cheek to icy cheek,
kiss, then shudder to discover
the heat waiting inside their mouths.

THE VOW

When the lover
goes, the vow though
broken remains, that
trace of eternity love
brings down among us
stays, to give
dignity to the suffering
and to intensify it.

THE ROOM

The door closes on pain and confusion.
The candle flame wavers from side to side
as though trying to break itself in half
to color the shadows too with living light.
The andante movement plays over and over
its many triplets, like farm dogs yapping
at a melody made of the gratification-cries
of cocks. I will not stay long.
Nothing in experience led me to imagine
having. Having is destroying, said
my version of the vow of impoverishment.
But here, in this brief, waxen light,
I have, and nothing is destroyed. The flute
that guttered those owl's notes into the waste hours
of childhood joins with the piano
and they play, *Being is having*. Having
may be nothing but the grace of the shell
moving without hesitation, with lively pride,
down the stubborn river of woe. At the far end,
a door no one dares open begins opening.
To go through it will awaken such regret
as only closing it behind can obliterate.
The candle flame's staggering makes the room
wobble and shift—matter itself, laughing.
I can't come back. I won't change.
I have the usual capacity for wanting
what may not even exist. Don't worry.

That is the dew wetting my face.
You see? Nothing that enters the room
can have only its own meaning ever again.

DIVINITY

When the man touches through
to the exact center of the woman,
he lies motionless, in equilibrium,
in absolute desire, at the threshold
of the world to which the Creator Spirit
knows the pass-whisper, and whispers it,
and his loving friend becomes his divinity.

LAST GODS

She sits naked on a rock
a few yards out in the water.
He stands on the shore,
also naked, picking blueberries.
She calls. He turns. She opens
her legs showing him her great beauty,
and smiles, a bow of lips
seeming to tie together
the ends of the earth.
Splashing her image
to pieces, he wades out
and stands before her, sunk
to the anklebones in leaf-mush
and bottom-slime—the intimacy
of the visible world. He puts
a berry in its shirt
of mist into her mouth.
She swallows it. He puts in another.
She swallows it. Over the lake
two swallows whim, juke, jink,
and when one snatches
an insect they both whirl up
and exult. He is swollen
not with ichor but with blood.
She takes him and sucks him
more swollen. He kneels, opens
the dark, vertical smile
linking heaven with the underearth

and licks her smoothest flesh more smooth.
On top of the rock they join.
Somewhere a frog moans, a crow screams.
The hair of their bodies
startles up. They cry
in the tongue of the last gods,
who refused to go,
chose death, and shuddered
in joy and shattered in pieces,
bequeathing their cries
into the human mouth. Now in the lake
two faces float, looking up
at a great maternal pine whose branches
open out in all directions
explaining everything.

FLOWER OF FIVE BLOSSOMS

Flower of five blossoms
I have brought you with me here
because you might not still be blossoming when I go back,
and because you might not blossom again.
I watched each of your buds swell up,
like water collected on a child's lid, about to plop,
or the catch in a throat that turns into a sob,
or in a tenor's throat, on some nights into a hundred sobs.
But as the buds
became these blossoms,
I am trying to learn: time suffered
is not necessarily time destroyed.
Outside, snow falls down in big pieces, like petals,
while in here, fire blossoms
out of wood and goes up in flames,
which are not *things dying* but just the *dying*.
Above them on the mantelpiece,
how calm your blossoms appear, austere and orderly, like the faces of
    singers,
but singing in silence, like the child
half-hidden by the pew, who dares only to think the hymns.
Phalaenopsis, sensual Orchidaceae,
sometimes, out of the corner of the eye, your blossoms perched on
    their twigs seem true to your name, "moth-like,"
and there, in the salep risen out of the pot of chipped bark, is the
    origin of your family name, ὄρχις, "testicle."
A few minutes ago, I put on a sonata by Brahms
("Brahms," nearly the sound dwelling on you forms in my mouth)

and I was standing at the mantelpiece
just as the slowest passage began, that moment
when the bow rests nearly immobile on the strings
—as mouths might, on mouths, in stillest kissing,
when a lip could be lying against a tooth in the other mouth, one
 can't say—
the bow's tremblings at what is about to happen
all that shakes any sound out of the strings at all,
and I turned and saw
what everyone else perhaps sees at once:
that in each blossom
the calyx's middle petal curves up
and flows over the mons veneris and spreads across the belly,
and the petal on either side rises over the thigh, one edge following
 the ridge of the pelvic bone, which is prominent, for she lies on
 her back,
and the two petals that are set back hold the roundness of her
 buttocks,
and at the center, in the little crown,
the clitoris leans, above
the vestibule opening into the center of being;
and I wanted to lean close,
without sound, with my lips
touching lightly one of your blossoms,
and find there, like a kiss that has a soft lick in it, like "blossoms,"
the name of this place and speak it.
That's what two keep trying to do,
over and over, at night,
singing,
sometimes together, sometimes alone—
but in a little while they forget, and think they haven't found it,
and what is mute and wet waits again to be sung.
As the sonata ends,

your blossoms fall more profoundly still
—their lavender streaks suddenly empty, like staff-lines before any
    notes have been entered—
have a portion of death in them,
and watch,
intent, unblinking,
like the white, hooded faces of cobras
risen up to mesmerize, or to fling themselves forward into the deadly
    kiss;
though each wears the headdress of Mary.
Or am I myself the spellbinder and the killer?
Alone here, I often find myself thinking of women—
and now your blossoms could stand for five of them—
any five, if I were to try to name them—
one could be she to whom I was married for many years,
or she who merely exchanged a few words with me, across a table,
    under the noise of the conversation of the others,
or that pale, laughing beauty I hugged at the dancing lessons, when
    we were fifteen,
and another could be the woman whose strict intelligence I revere,
    whom I kiss on the forehead, a quarter inch away from the brain,
    the way Plato kissed,
and then the fifth blossom would be my mother, risen up at my
    bedside, wanting to please, but having, the next day or another,
    to crush—
strange,
for I began by speaking of sexual resemblance,
but not strange, for it was as a sexual creature she seized me into
    existence,
it was through her vagina, trespassed by a man one way, transpierced
    by three babies the other,
I was dragged out alive, into the dead
of winter—a day

perhaps like this day, sixty years later, when out there earth
draws down on top of herself yet another of her freezing sleeping
    clothes,
but underneath is awakening . . .
besoming . . . blowsining . . . blissamous . . .
and in here, at the mantelpiece,
bending close to you, praying to you almost, standing almost in
    flames,
I wonder
what can come of these minutes,
each a hard inner tumbling, as when a key nearly won't turn,
or the note of a piano, clattered or stroked, ringing.
Everyone knows
everything sings and dies.
But it could be, too, everything dies and sings,
and a life is the interlude
when, still humming, we can look up, gawk about, imagine whatever,
    say it,
topple back into singing.
Oh first our voice be done, and then, before and afterwards and all
    around it, that singing.

FAREWELL

after Haydn's Symphony in F-sharp Minor

for Paul Zweig (1935–1984)

The last adagio begins.
Soon a violinist gets up and walks out.
Two cellists follow, bows erect, cellos dangling.
The flutist leaves lifting the flute high to honor it for blowing
    during all that continuous rubbing.
The bassoonist goes, then the bass fiddler.
The fortepiano player abandons the black, closeted contraption and
    walks away shaking her fingertips.
The orchestra disappears—
by ones, the way we wash up on this unmusical shore,
and by twos, the way we enter the ark where the world goes on
    beginning.
Before leaving each player blows
the glimmer off the music-stand candle,
where fireweed, dense blazing star, flame azalea stored it summers
    ago,
puffing that quantity of darkness into the hall
and the same portion of light
into the elsewhere where the players reassemble and wait
for the oboist to come with her reliable A,
as first light arrives in a beech and hemlock forest,
setting the birds sounding their chaotic vowels,
so they can tune,
and then play
the phrases inside flames wobbling on top of stalks in the field,

53

and in fireflies' greenish sparks of grass-sex,
and in gnats whining past in a spectral bunch,
and in crickets who would saw themselves apart to sing,
and in the golden finch perched in the mountain ash, whose roots
    push into the mouths of the emptied singers.
Now all the players have gone but two violinists,
who sit half facing each other, friends who have figured out what
    they have figured out by sounding it upon the other,
and scathe the final phrases.
By ones and twos, our powers rise and go,
to lie jangled up in stacks
in woodsheds waiting until a new winter
to spring again in crackling orange voices; and only two are left.
In the darkness above the stage I imagine
the face of my old friend Paul Zweig
—who went away, his powers intact, into Eternity's Woods alone,
    under a double singing of birds—
looking down and saying something like,
"Let the limits of knowing stretch and diaphanise:
knowledge increasing into ignorance gives the falling-trajectory its
    grace."
The bow-hairs still cast dust on the bruised wood.
Everything on earth, born
only moments ago, abruptly tips over
and is dragged by mistake into the chaotic inevitable.
Goodbye, dear friend.
Even the meantime, which is the holy time
of being on earth in overlapping lifetimes, ends.
This is one of its endings.
The violinists scrape one more time,
the last of the adagio flies out through the f-holes.
The audience straggles from the hall and at once disappears.
For myself I go on foot on Seventh Avenue

down to the little, bent streets of the West Village.
From ahead of me comes the *hic* of somebody drunk
and then the *nunc* of his head bumping against a telephone pole.

PART IV

WHEN ONE HAS LIVED
A LONG TIME ALONE

I

When one has lived a long time alone,
one refrains from swatting the fly
and lets him go, and one hesitates to strike
the mosquito, though more than willing to slap
the flesh under her, and one lifts the toad
from the pit too deep to hop out of
and carries him to the grass, without minding
the poisoned urine he slicks his body with,
and one envelops, in a towel, the swift
who fell down the chimney and knocks herself
against window glass and releases her outside
and watches her fly free, a life line flung at reality,
when one has lived a long time alone.

2

When one has lived a long time alone,
one grabs the snake behind the head
and holds him until he stops trying to stick
the orange tongue—which splits at the end
into two black filaments and jumps out
like a fire-eater's belches and has little
in common with the pimpled pink lump that shapes
sounds and sleeps inside the human mouth—
into one's flesh, and clamps it between his jaws,
letting the gaudy tips show, as children do
when concentrating, and as very likely
one does oneself, without knowing it,
when one has lived a long time alone.

3

When one has lived a long time alone,
among regrets so immense the past occupies
nearly all the room there is in consciousness,
one notices in the snake's eyes, which look back
without giving any less attention to the future,
the first coating of the opaque, milky-blue
leucoma snakes get when about to throw their skins
and become new—meanwhile continuing,
of course, to grow old—the same *bleu passé*
that bleaches the corneas of the blue-eyed
when they lie back at the end and look for heaven,
a fading one knows means they will never find it
when one has lived a long time alone.

4

When one has lived a long time alone,
one holds the snake near the loudspeaker disgorging
gorgeous sound and watches him crook
his forepart into four right angles,
as though trying to slow down the music
flowing through him, in order to absorb it
like milk of paradise into the flesh,
until a glimmering appears at his mouth,
such a drop of intense fluid as, among humans,
could form after long exciting at the tip
of the penis, and as he straightens himself out
he has the pathos one finds in the penis,
when one has lived a long time alóne.

5

When one has lived a long time alone,
one falls to poring upon a creature,
contrasting its eternity's-face to one's own
full of hours, taking note of each difference,
exaggerating it, making it everything,
until the other is utterly other, and then,
with hard effort, possibly with tongue sticking out,
going back over each difference once again
and canceling it, seeing nothing now
but likeness, until . . . half an hour later
one starts awake, taken aback at how eagerly
one drops off into the happiness of kinship,
when one has lived a long time alone.

6

When one has lived a long time alone
and listens at morning to mourning doves
sound their kyrie eleison, or the small thing
spiritualized upon a twig cry, "pewit-phoebe!"
or at midday grasshoppers scratch the thighs'
needfire awake, or peabody birds send schoolboys'
whistlings across the field, and at dusk, undamped,
unforgiving chinks, as from marble cutters' chisels,
or at nightfall polliwogs just burst into frogs
raise their ave verum corpus—listens to those
who hop or fly call down upon us the mercy
of other tongues—one hears them as inner voices,
when one has lived a long time alone.

7

When one has lived a long time alone,
one knows that consciousness consummates,
and as the conscious one among these others
uttering their compulsory cries of being here—
the least flycatcher witching up "che-bec!"
or red-headed woodpecker clanging out his music
from a metal drainpipe, or ruffed grouse drumming
"thrump thrump thrump thrump-thrump-
thrump-thrump-rup-rup-rup-rup-rup-r-r-r-r-r"
deep in the woods, all of them in time's unfolding
trying to cry themselves into self-knowing—
one knows one is here to hear them into shining,
when one has lived a long time alone.

8

When one has lived a long time alone,
one likes alike the pig, who brooks no deferment
of gratification, and the porcupine, or thorned pig,
who enters the cellar but not the house itself
because of eating down the cellar stairs on the way up,
and one likes the worm, who by bunching herself together
and expanding works her way through the ground,
no less than the butterfly, who totters full of worry
among the day lilies, as they darken,
and more and more one finds one likes
any other species better than one's own,
which has gone amok, making one self-estranged,
when one has lived a long time alone.

9

When one has lived a long time alone,
sour, misanthropic, one fits to one's defiance
the satanic boast, *It is better to reign
in hell than to submit on earth*, and forgets
one's kind—the way by now the snake does,
who stops trying to get to the floor and lingers
all across one's body, slumping into its contours,
adopting its temperature—and abandons hope
of the sweetness of friendship or love,
before long can barely remember what they are,
and covets the stillness in inorganic matter,
in a self-dissolution one may not know how to halt,
when one has lived a long time alone.

IO

When one has lived a long time alone,
and the hermit thrush calls and there is an answer,
and the bullfrog head half out of water repeats
the sexual cantillations of his first spring,
and the snake lowers himself over the threshold
and disappears among the stones, one sees
they all live to mate with their kind, and one knows,
after a long time of solitude, after the many steps taken
away from one's kind, toward the kingdom of strangers,
the hard prayer inside one's own singing
is to come back, if one can, to one's own,
a world almost lost, in the exile that deepens,
when one has lived a long time alone.

II

When one has lived a long time alone,
one wants to live again among men and women,
to return to that place where one's ties with the human
broke, where the disquiet of death and now also
of history glimmers its firelight on faces,
where the gaze of the new baby looks past the gaze
of the great granny, and where lovers speak,
on lips blowsy from kissing, that language
the same in each mouth, and like birds at daybreak
blether the song that is both earth's and heaven's,
until the sun has risen, and they stand
in a halo of being made one: kingdom come,
when one has lived a long time alone.

A NOTE ABOUT THE AUTHOR

GALWAY KINNELL lives in Vermont and New York City. He has been the director of an adult education program in Chicago, a journalist in Iran, and a field worker for the Congress of Racial Equality in Louisiana. During the past twenty years he has taught poetry at colleges and universities in this country and in France and Australia. His *Selected Poems*, published in 1982, won both the National Book Award and the Pulitzer Prize. A former MacArthur Fellow, Galway Kinnell is State Poet of Vermont and Samuel F. B. Morse Professor of Arts and Science at New York University.

A NOTE ON THE TYPE

The text of this book is set in Linotype Garamond No. 3. It is not a true copy of any of the designs of Claude Garamond (1480–1561), but an adaptation of his types, which set the European standard for two centuries. It probably owes as much to the designs of Jean Jannon, a Protestant printer working in Sedan in the early seventeenth century, who had worked with Garamond's romans earlier, in Paris, and who was denied their use because of the Catholic censorship. Jannon's matrices came into the possession of the Imprimerie Nationale, where they were thought to be by Garamond himself, and so described when the Imprimerie revived the type in 1900. This particular version is based on an adaptation by Morris Fuller Benton.

Composition, printing and binding by
Heritage Printers, Charlotte, North Carolina.